ERSIONS!

AV-8
HARRIER

in detail & scale

Don Linn

TAB TAB BOOKS Inc.
Blue Ridge Summit, PA

Airlife Publishing Ltd.
England

Copyright © 1988 BY DETAIL & SCALE. INC.

All rights reserved. No part of this publication may be reproduced in any form, stored in a retrieval system, or transmitted by any means, electronic, mechanical, or otherwise, except in a review, without the written consent of Detail & Scale, Inc.

This book is a product of Detail & Scale, Inc., which has sole responsibility for the contents and layout, except that all contributors are responsible for the security clearance and copyright release or all materials submitted. Published and distributed in the United States by TAB BOOKS Inc. and in Great Britain and Europe by Airlife Publishing Ltd.

Don Spering/AIR
David F. Brown
Peter H. Becker
Dana Bell
Jim Sullivan
Bert Kinzey

Norm Taylor
Jerry Geer
Steve Sauve
Tom Chee
Steve VanDerryt

C.H. Pilkington
Public Affairs Office, MCAS Cherry Point
McDonnell Douglas
Bill Frierson, PAO
NAS Patuxent River
British Aerospace

GYSGT Bill Brown, USMC
GYSGT Ed Miranda, USMC
Dick Starinchak
Jim Galloway
William D. Spidle

EDITED BY BERT KINZEY

Most photographs in this book are credited to their contributors. Photos with no credit indicated were taken by the author.

Special Acknowledgment

The author wishes to extend a special thanks to the members of Delaware Valley Scale Modelers (Philadelphia) Chapter, IPMS/USA, for their help in building the Harrier models and writing the kit reviews for each that appear in the modeling section of this book. Thanks guys! They are:

Len Salatti
Ed Miranda
Ralph Ratcliffe
Marin Ennis

Paul Florence
George Waeckel, Jr.
Walter G. Weich
Reggie Rogers

FIRST EDITION
FIRST PRINTING

Published in United States by

TAB BOOKS Inc.
Blue Ridge Summit, PA 17294-0214

Library of Congress Cataloging
in Publication Data

Linn, Don, 1945-
AV-8 Harrier.

(Detail & Scale : vol. 28)
1. Harrier (Jet fighter plane) I. Title.
UG1252.F5L55 1988 623.74'64 87-26780
ISBN 0-8306-8038-1 (pbk. : v. 1)

First published in Great Britain in 1988
by Airlife Publishing Ltd.
7 St. John's Hill, Shrewsbury, SY1 1JE

British Library Cataloging In
Publication Data

Linn, Don
AV-8 Harrier. - (Detail and scale series; v.28).
Part 1: U.S.M.C. Versions
1. Harrier (Jet fighter plane)
I. Title II. Series
623.74'64   UG1242.F5
ISBN 1-85310-605-4

Questions regarding the content of this book
should be addressed to:

Reader Inquiry Branch
TAB BOOKS Inc.
Blue Ridge Summit, PA 17294-0214

Front cover: This AV-8B Harrier II is loaded with 500-pound, Mk-82 Snakeye bombs, and was photographed near MCAS Yuma during an October 1985 training flight. *(McDonnell Douglas)*

Rear cover: A TAV-8A two-seat Harrier is seen here during the first aerial refueling of a TAV-8A in March 1987. The aircraft was on a cross-country flight to NAS Fallon, Nevada.

INTRODUCTION

An AV-8A from VMA-513 is seen here performing a vertical takeoff. Two Sidewinder missiles and two drop tanks are fitted to the underwing pylons. (BAe)

V/STOL--the letters stand for Vertical/Short TakeOff and Landing. It is an idea that has been tried many times, but one that has almost always met with failure or very limited success when it has been tried on a fixed-wing aircraft. This book is about the AV-8 Harrier, which is undoubtedly the most successful V/STOL aircraft ever flown. Originally designed by the British, it has long been used by the United States Marines in the form of the AV-8A, TAV-8A, and AV-8C. A new version has recently become operational in the form of the AV-8B, which is produced by McDonnell Douglas.

Don Linn has written a number of aviation books and articles, to include The F-18 Hornet in Detail & Scale, that became one of the more successful titles in the Detail & Scale series. With this volume he begins a two-part look at the Harrier, which is one of only two operational military jet aircraft in service today that have a V/STOL capability. The other is the Yak-36 FORGER that is produced by the Soviet Union. In this first part, Don covers all versions of the Harrier that have been used by the United States. This includes the AV-8A, TAV-8A, AV-8B, AV-8C, TAV-8B, and the proposed new night attack version of the Harrier. The foreign versions will be covered in the second part that is scheduled for a future Detail & Scale volume.

As is the case with all books in this series, the focus is on the many details of the aircraft. Photographs and drawings show details of the cockpits, landing gear, ordnance, and much more. Differences between the prototypes and each of the production versions are explained and illustrated. The five-view drawings are of the AV-8B, and were drawn specifically for this book by Dana Bell, an

author and illustrator who has both written and done drawings for Detail & Scale in the past. Supplemental views are provided for the AV-8A and TAV-8A.

An interesting history is included that traces the design and development of the AV-8A and AV-8B. It also describes the modifications that were incorporated to produce the AV-8C. Development of the TAV-8B and the proposed new Harrier night attack version is also outlined. Since the AV-8B is such a new aircraft, and is still having modifications and improvements added to it, every attempt was made to get all of the information and photographs presented in this book as up-to-date as possible.

The usual modelers section reviews all presently available kits of the versions of the Harrier that are covered in this publication. The illustrated models were built by the Philadelphia Chapter of IPMS/USA, and Detail & Scale acknowledges and thanks them for their contributions to this book. A listing of decals for these kits is also provided.

The Harrier is the only combat aircraft currently serving with U.S. forces that traces its design back to another country. In this sense it is unique, and it was the first truly successful V/STOL aircraft in the world to go into full production. Many experts today believe that V/STOL aircraft will become the rule, rather than the exception, in the future. Whether or not this is true remains to be seen, but, regardless, the Harrier has made an important and indelible mark on aviation history. Detail & Scale is pleased to have Don Linn provide this close-up and detailed look at this unusual aircraft.

THE V/STOL CONCEPT

The 100th Production AV-8B was delivered to VMA-542 with much ceremony on December 29, 1987.

(Spering/AIR)

On April 15, 1971, the first US Marine Corps Harrier squadron was formed. It is a marriage that has endured almost twenty years, and during that time the Harrier has evolved from the early AV-8A produced by British Aerospace, then Hawker Siddeley, to the new McDonnell Douglas AV-8B Harrier II. And, like any marriage, there have been good times and bad. It has been a fight, both within the Marine Corps and the Department of Defense, to keep the Harrier from the very beginning. It has also been a political battle as well, but the Harrier has survived it all, and is expected to be a major asset in Marine Corps aviation into the next century.

The Harrier is unique in its design and capabilities, and although in its early form, namely the AV-8A, it lacked range and payload capability, its V/STOL characteristics proved to be a greater offsetting value. The design is of British origin, but it captured the eye of the Marines early in its development when first deployed by the RAF's No. 1 Squadron in July 1969. The ability to take off like a helicopter and transition to conventional flight was the best of both worlds, and the Marines recognized this. It was the perfect asset for close air support, a role the Marines knew and excelled in. The problem was buying a military fighter from a foreign government, something that had not occurred since the 1930s. Political leaders in the U.S. Congress were opposed to the purchase, but fortunately wiser minds prevailed. With all its good points and bad, the Harrier is ideally suited for the role of close air support, and, behind the lines, its V/STOL capabilities permit a quick response. The new AV-8B can only enhance those capabilities with greater range and

payload. The Harrier has changed and evolved over the past twenty years, and has lead the way for other V/STOL aircraft that are being designed today.

The idea for a V/STOL (Vertical/Short Takeoff and Landing) fighter aircraft is not new. The need for a military aircraft that can take off vertically and transition to conventional flight was dreamed of from the earliest days of military aviation. When military aircraft became viable threats to opposing sides during World War I, their aerodromes became targets. If the enemy was capable of knocking out the airfields, prohibiting the fighters and bombers from taking off, a great military objective was accomplished. This led to the search for a practical military aircraft that did not need airfields or runways from which to take off or land. If such an aircraft could be developed, a great tactical military advantage could be achieved.

The first of such aircraft were airships, the giant gas bags in the sky that fell prey to smaller fighters. The size, slow speed, and lack of maneuverability prevented these from being anything more than high flying observation platforms. Helicopters were the next great advancement in an attempt to produce a V/STOL aircraft. Their success is evident, but also somewhat limited. Helicopter gunships are a close second to Harriers, but still lack that unique quality that only the Harrier has so far been able to achieve. That is to be a legitimate fixed-wing aircraft that can take off and land vertically, transition to conventional flight, and still carry a respectable warload. This dream of a practical military V/STOL aircraft has been realized in the Harrier.

DEVELOPMENTAL HISTORY

The Hawker P.1127 was the forerunner to today's Harrier. (BAe)

During the decade of the 1950s, military jet aircraft, and especially naval jet fighter and attack aircraft, had progressed from the infancy of jets, such as the McDonnell FH-1 Phantom and North American FJ-1 Fury, to LTV's F-8 Crusader and the McDonnell Douglas A-4 Skyhawk. It was a fast and dramatic period of growth, but often a period not really appreciated today. We tend not to realize that World War II, with its P-51 Mustangs and F4U Corsairs, had ended in the previous five short years. Yet the 1950s was a time when jets were born and matured, and this led the way for even greater developments in the 1960s.

The F-4 Phantom, now completing thirty years of continuous military service, was a product of the 1950s, having been designed and developed during the second half of that decade. It entered squadron service in 1961. It was also during that same period in time that a new aircraft design, then being developed by Hawker Aircraft (before it became Hawker Siddeley and eventually British Aerospace) would prove to be as revolutionary to aviation as the Wright Flyer.

Hawker P.1127

The Hawker project that was given the design number P.1127 was the forerunner of today's AV-8B Harrier II. In

practical terms it was a straightforward aircraft design that overcame all the pitfalls that befell the search for a workable V/STOL design. It also gave Hawker the lead in 1962 when NATO issued NMBR.3 in June of that year. NMBR.3 (NATO Military Basic Requirement) was a design requirement for a vertical-takeoff-strike-reconnaissance aircraft that was intended to equip NATO's air arms in the late 1960s, replacing the Hawker Hunter and Fiat G.91 then serving in most of NATO's air forces.

A press release issued by Hawker on November 25, 1960, said in part, "... the P.1127 has successfully completed the initial hovering trials which started on October 25. These concluded with a number of hovering flights free of any ground restraints . . . ." The first practical V/STOL aircraft was born! Although the P.1127 was designed and developed as a private venture by Hawker, the British Ministry of Aviation became actively interested and issued a contract for the production of two prototype aircraft of the P.1127 design. A total of six P.1127s would eventually be built.

This contract for two prototype P.1127 aircraft issued by the Ministry of Aviation was let almost two full years before NATO's NMBR.3 was presented to the free world's leading aircraft industries. This gave Hawker Siddeley a

The first of the P.1127 Kestrels assigned to the Tripartite Evaluation Squadron displays its special segmented roundel.
(BAe)

definite advantage in development work with a full scale prototype before the other aircraft builders even began design work. Just the same, the competition was fierce as each manufacturer sought to win this financially lucrative contract. However, the future would find this contract to be fraught with political differences, and in fact never really materialized to be the financial boom it was expected to be.

In the meantime Hawker Siddeley continued with the development work and building of the two new P.1127 prototypes under the agreement with the Ministry of Aviation. The first P.1127 was given the registration number XP831, and the five additional P.1127s that would follow carried the registration numbers XP836, XP972, XP976, XP980 and XP984. The first P.1127 was, by 1961, proving to be a greater success than originally anticipated. But the key to its success must equally be shared between Hawker's design and the power plant developed by Bristol Siddeley. Their BS.53 engine, later to be named Pegasus, was the heart of the P.1127.

The BS.53 was a completely new front fan turbo-fan engine. Its exhaust flow was divided between two pairs of nozzles which could be rotated to deflect the exhaust flow aft for thrust, down for lift, or to intermediate positions for a combination of both thrust and lift. The BS.53

produced 12,000 lbs. of thrust, considerably less than the Rolls Royce Pegasus in the AV-8B that produces 23,000 lbs. of thrust. But, although the engine in the AV-8B can produce greater thrust than in the original BS.53, the engine design is basically the same. Bristol's BS.53 design was the breakthrough that made the P.1127 possible.

The first setback in the P.1127 program occurred on December 14, 1961, when the second prototype, XP836, crashed. The cause of the crash was a defective nozzle that was lost in flight during a high speed, low level flight near Yeovilton. Bill Bedford, Hawker's Chief Test Pilot, was flying XP836, which had joined the test program six months earlier in July. When he experienced engine trouble, he elected to make an emergency landing at the nearby Royal Navy airfield at Yeovilton. On approach, XP836 became uncontrollable, forcing Bedford to eject while still at a safe altitude to do so. The resulting crash of the P.1127 was a total loss. The cause of the mishap was due to the front port nozzle falling off, perhaps due to excessive stress. The nozzles were, up to that time, made of fiberglass, but even before this accident a decision had been made to replace the fiberglass nozzles with those made of steel.

The second crash of a P.1127 occurred at the 1963

AV-8A Harriers are shown here on the assembly line at Hawker Siddeley. (BAe)

Paris Air Show at Le Bourget. The Paris Air Show is known the world over as the show place of aviation technology, a place where manufacturers can show off their latest aircraft designs. It is also a place where potential buyers come to see what is new. Hawker decided to send two of their new P.1127s to Le Bourget to demonstrate their breakthrough in V/STOL technology. Bill Bedford was flying the original P.1127, XP831, demonstrating its ability to hover and transition to conventional flight, all to the delight of those watching. It was a truly impressive demonstration. At the conclusion of his performance, Bedford came in for a vertical landing near the French President's viewing platform when XP831 suddenly lost lift and dropped heavily to the ground. Bedford emerged shaken, but unhurt. XP831 was badly damaged. The cause of the crash was later traced to a dirt blockage in the pressure reducing valve. This caused a failure in the air motors that control the rotation of the exhaust nozzles. The P.1127 was repaired and continued in the test program. After its retirement it was sent to the Royal Air Force Museum at Henden where it remains today.

The P.1127s continued flight trials at the Royal Air Force Establishments at Bedford, Farnborough, and Bascombe Down. The success of the program was evident. Six P.1127s were built and proved Hawker's V/STOL concept to be a practical approach for a military application to a vertical takeoff and landing fighter. Bristol, the builder of the BS.53 engine, had progressed from the original 12,000 lbs. of thrust to a Pegasus 5 engine of 15,500 lbs. of thrust by September 1963. The P.1127 test program was nearing an end by this time, and a new stage in the Harrier's evolution was beginning.

KESTREL (XV-6)

Following the success of the P.1127, and the failure of any other workable V/STOL design, the United States, West Germany, and Britain worked together in a collaborative effort to jointly fund the cost of nine V/STOL aircraft based on the Hawker design. This agreement, to be known officially as the Tripartite Agreement, was signed in Paris on January 16, 1963. The three nations would share equally in the cost of the manufacture of nine aircraft, their developmental and operational cost, and of a squadron of pilots and related personnel from the three countries partied to the agreement.

While the nine new developmental aircraft were being built, the pilots selected for this program began training in the original P.1127s. The first of the new developmental aircraft began taxiing trials at Dunsfold on March 5, 1964, and finally made its first flight two days later on March 7. This new V/STOL aircraft was given the official designation FGA Mk.1 (Fighter, Ground Attack), and the name Kestrel was adopted. The Kestrel strongly resembled its predecessor in size and outline, and benefitted from the experience gained in the P.1127. However, it differed from the original with a larger tailplane for improved longitudinal stability, a slight increase of chord in the outer wing panels, steamlined wing tips with faired outriggers, a new intake fairing, and a new nose-mounted camera. A new Pegasus 5 with 18,000 lbs. of thrust was installed in the first Kestrels, but work on a new Pegasus 6 with greater thrust was under development and would be installed in later production models. Performance of the Kestrel was quite spectacular for its day, and, even by today's standards, it could reach a maximum speed of Mach .87 at sea level, attain Mach 1 in a shallow dive, and fly 70 mph sideways and 30 mph backwards!

One of the Kestrels, redesignated XV-6, served with the USAF following the Tripartite Evaluation trials. (AAHS)

This AV-8A, still bearing its RAF serial XV742, was used by the Marines to evaluate the Harrier's capabilities. It is armed with four Matra rocket pods, two Aden gun pods, and a 1000-pound bomb. (BAe)

The squadron was known as the Tripartite Evaluation Squadron, or TES as it was commonly called at the time. It was commanded by Wing Commander David Scrimgeour, RAF, with two deputy commanders, Col. Gerhard F. Barkhorn, Luftwaffe, and CDR. J.J. Tyson, USN. Formed at the Central Fighter Establishment, West Raynham, on October 15, 1964, the Tripartite Evaluation Squadron was authorized to use a special segmented roundel equally divided with the three countries' national insignias. More importantly, the squadron was tasked with evaluating the Kestrel FGA Mk.1 and its unique V/STOL capabilities. The squadron was responsible for six major evaluation points: suitability of V/STOL aircraft for operations in the field, comparison of various methods of takeoff and landing, flight operating procedures and techniques, jet-borne operations, instrument flight, and night flying.

The Tripartite Evaluation Squadron worked for eleven short months gathering data for further evaluation and study. During that time 938 takeoffs and landings were completed, and 1,200 sorties were flown, accumulating 585 flight hours. One Kestrel, XS696, was lost during a short takeoff accident involving one of the US Army pilots assigned to the squadron. This aircraft was not replaced, leaving the test program to continue with only eight Kes-

trels. A second Kestrel, XS689, was also involved in a crash, but was repaired and returned to the squadron after several weeks.

By all standards, the trials completed by the Tripartite Evaluation Squadron were a success. More importantly, it proved the practicality of Hawker's V/STOL concept and design. So it was with some surprise that at the conclusion of the Tripartite Evaluation, Germany did not elect to exercise its option to continue flight trials with their three Kestrels used in the Tripartite Evaluation. Instead, Germany's three Kestrels, along with the two remaining assigned to the United States, plus one additional Kestrel from the RAF, were sent to the United States for further trials in the Air Force, Navy, and Army Tri-Service evaluation.

The Tripartite Evaluation trials ended in January 1966. The results of all the data collected, the sorties flown, and the flight hours provided a great deal of information. But in the end, Germany decided against any further participation in Hawker's V/STOL project. The United States was unsure and continued additional testing, but the RAF knew what the Kestrel and P.1127 meant, although there was considerable political resistance to this Hawker project.

THE HARRIER

AV-8As operated off HMS Hermes during the Royal Navy carrier's 1978 visit to the U.S. It sailed from Mayport, Florida, to Norfolk, Virginia.   *(HMS Hermes)*

Following the success of the Tripartite Evaluation Squadron and the flight trials of the FGA Mk.1 Kestrel in 1965, RAF planners issued Air Staff Requirement 384 covering a production version of the FGA Mk.1 Kestrel. This staff requirement specified operational requirements for combined ground attack and reconnaissance roles. In 1967 this aircraft would officially be designated Harrier GR Mk.1.

Production of the GR Mk.1 prototype began almost immediately, with the first flight taking place on August 31, 1966, and the first flight of the production Harrier being made December 28, 1968. However, first delivery of production Harriers did not occur until April 1969. It was nearly ten years from the date of the first flight of the P.1127 to active squadron service with the RAF.

The GR Mk.1 differed greatly from the Kestrel, although outward appearances are similar. In fact, the performance of the Harrier was significantly upgraded

over the Kestrel's to meet the demands of a modern fighter. The biggest improvement was in the new Pegasus 6, with its all titanium fan. It had a revised combustion system with water ejection, and was rated at 19,000 lbs. of thrust. Armament capabilities were equally enhanced by two 30mm Aden gun pods fitted to the undersides, four wing hardpoints, plus one centerline hardpoint between the Aden gun pods. For extended flight, a refueling probe was added, and, for ferry flights, extended bolt-on wing-tips could be added. The cockpit was changed, and included a Ferranti inertial navigation/attack system (INAS) and a Smiths head-up display (HUD).

For the reconnaissance role, an F95 camera was mounted in the nose, plus additional cameras were contained in a belly pod usually carried between the two Aden guns. Weapons systems certified for the Harrier were compatible with other fighter/attack aircraft serving in the RAF and NATO.

USMC SERVICE

The first production AV-8A, 158384, served with the first USMC Harrier squadron, VMA-513, at MCAS Beaufort, South Carolina, on June 15, 1972. (Spering/AIR)

USMC AV-8A

As the first RAF Harriers were entering squadron service in 1969, the Marines were expressing strong interest in its V/STOL capabilities and all-around performance. The Harrier was ideally suited for the Marine's close support requirements with its ability to operate from unimproved sites or from ships. Thus, in 1970, an order for 102 single-seat Harriers and eight two-seat trainers were ordered. These were given the USMC designation AV-8A and TAV-8A, respectively. The order called for the first twelve AV-8As to be delivered in 1970, but even before this initial order was placed, politics entered the picture rather quickly. During the 1969 Fiscal Year Budget Debates, the U.S. Congress wanted a substantial number of these Harriers, if not all, to be built in the United States. There was strong resentment against buying a foreign

The two Aden guns are clearly visible on this AV-8A from VMA-542. The photograph was taken at MCAS Cherry Point in 1976. (Sullivan)

military aircraft, mainly because it would result in a loss of jobs and money in the U.S. aircraft industry. An agreement was finally reached whereby Hawker Siddeley would license a U.S. company to build the Harrier. In the end, a fifteen-year licensing agreement was consummated with McDonnell Douglas to produce Harriers. This agreement granted McDonnell Douglas exclusive rights for the sale and manufacture of the Harrier and of future Harrier derivatives. This was an important part of the agreement led to the development of the AV-8B, but of course the AV-8B was not even a bright spark in McAir's future at that time. This agreement also provided for a mutual exchange of V/STOL technology based on the Harrier's vectored thrust configuration.

It is interesting to note that after this outcry from Congress and the resulting licensing agreement between McAir and Hawker Siddeley, no AV-8As were ever produced in the United States. This is mainly due to the procrastination of Congress to approve the necessary funds for the step-by-step transfer of Harrier production from Hawker Siddeley to McDonnell Douglas. Hawker Siddeley had been delivering small batches of AV-8As to the Marines to meet their contract commitment, and, as each Fiscal Year passed without funding for this transfer of technology, the total number of Harriers on order dwindled to a point where it was not economically feasible to build Harriers at McDonnell Douglas. The entire fleet of 102 AV-8As and eight two-seat TAV-8A Harriers, was produced by Hawker Siddeley. The last Harrier delivered over this five year period was received by the Marines in 1976.

The AV-8A, as purchased by the Marines, is similar in most respects to the RAF GR.1. The AV-8A was powered by a Rolls Royce Pegasus Mk.103 rated at 21,500 lbs. of thrust, the former Bristol Engine Company having been acquired by Rolls Royce by this time. This engine was later designated F402-RR-401 by the Department of Defense.

Aside from the engine difference and a back-up manual fuel control system, other differences included U.S.-built avionics and flight control systems, and weapons systems that were compatible with U.S. military ordnance. Otherwise, even the external camouflage was the same as applied to RAF Harriers.

AV-8A Harriers served with three attack squadrons and one training squadron from September 1970 to July 1986, when the last AV-8A was retired.

AV-8A SQUADRONS	TAIL CODES
VMA-513	WF
VMA-542	WH
VMA-231	CG
VMAT-203	KD

102 AV-8A BuNos

158384-158395	159230-159259
158694-158711	159366-159377
158948-158977	

This AV-8A is from VMA-542, The Flying Tigers, and has a yellow and black tiger stripe rudder. It was photographed at MCAS Cherry Point on April 22, 1977. *(Sullivan)*

The blue rudder and nose number are difficult to see on this AV-8A from VMA-513, Det. A. The rudder stars are white. This photo was taken at Malstrom AFB during October 1976. *(Swanberg via Geer)*

This AV-8A was assigned to the Harrier training squadron, VMAT-203, at Cherry Point in 1978.

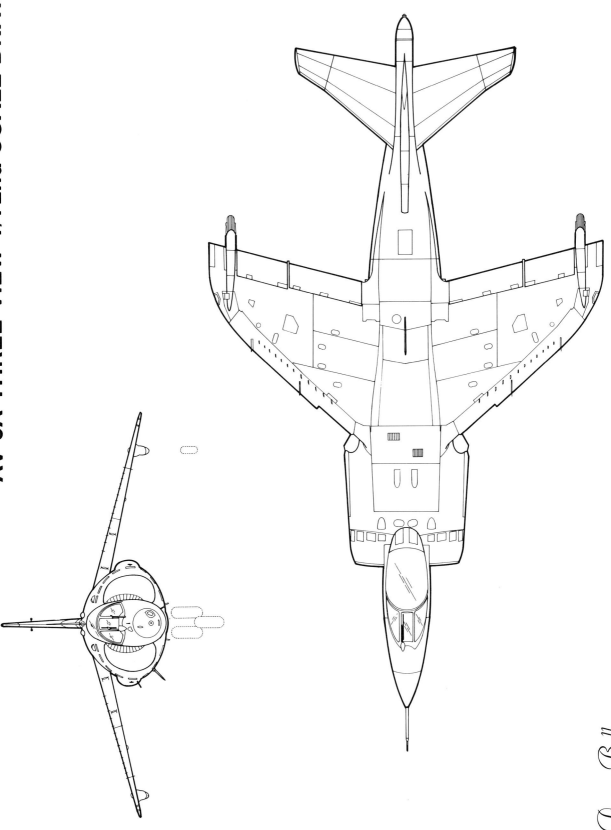

Dana Bell

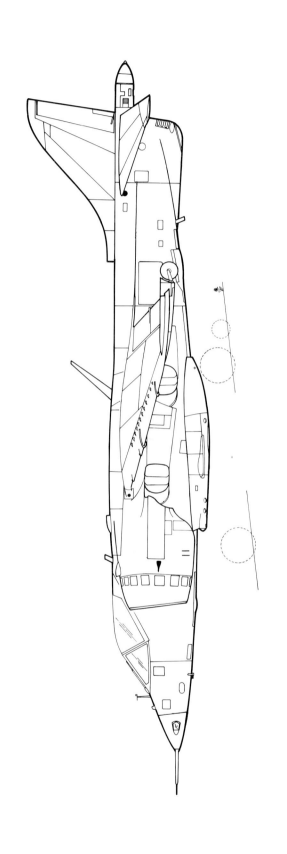

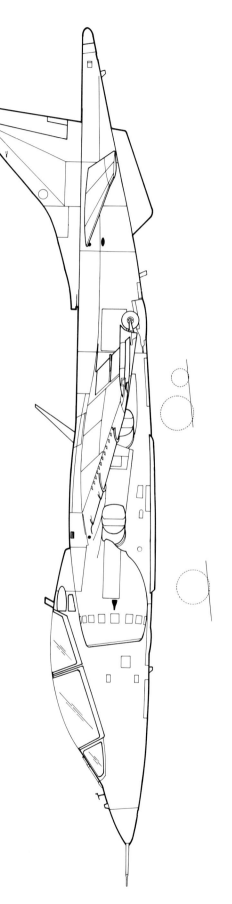

TAV-8A LEFT SIDE VIEW

Dana Bell

Above left: The deck crew is performing preflight checks on this AV-8A from VMA-231 during a 1976 Med cruise aboard USS Franklin D. Roosevelt. (USN)

Above right: A Harrier pilot checks the ram air turbine on this AV-8A from VMA-542 during a 1979 Med cruise aboard USS Iwo Jima, LPH-2. (USN)

The small size of the AV-8A is evident when compared to this A-7. (USN)

AV-8A DETAILS

Details of the right rear exhaust nozzle are seen here.

The right front exhaust nozzle is pictured here. Note the angle indicators painted on the side of the fuselage.

The AV-8A's tail cone is shown in this photograph that was taken from the right.

A 300-gallon drop tank is shown attached to the right inboard pylon.

The left formation light and fire access hole are located at the wing root. A similar arrangement is on the opposite side.

This is a close-up of the formation light on the right wing tip.

LANDING GEAR

Nose gear from the right

Rear main landing gear from the left

Left outrigger wheel detail

Left outrigger gear from behind

VIFFing

The one thing that makes the Harrier unique among all other aircraft, civil or military, is its ability to take off and land vertically. With the exception of helicopters, a few other experimental aircraft types, and the Russian Yak 36 Forger VTOL fighter, no other aircraft can perform like the Harrier. Taking this special feature one step further is VIFFing, an acronym derived from Vectoring in Forward Flight.

Vectoring in forward flight was discovered early in the Harrier's development, and, in simplest terms, it means to vector the four exhaust nozzles to the down position while flying forward, thus stopping the Harrier in mid-flight. One can only imagine the look on the face of the first pilot to engage a Harrier in a dogfight, and after getting into firing position on his tail, have the Harrier pilot change the direction of the exhaust nozzles to the down position. This would stop the Harrier in mid-flight, causing the pursuer to fly by. The Harrier pilot then would change the direction of the nozzles to forward flight and lock on to the tail of the pursuer. The hunter becomes the hunted!

The nozzle controls are located on the left console near the throttle. A single nozzle control lever is used to select the position with all four nozzles synchronized to work in unison. The pilot can select the nozzle position he desires for either VIFFing, short takeoff and landings, or for hovering.

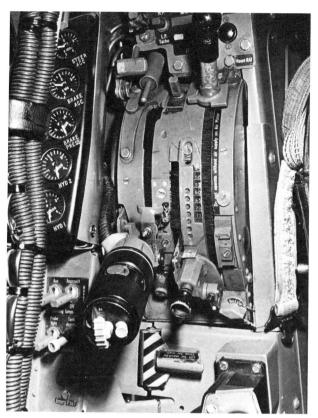

Throttle and nozzle controls in the AV-8A   *(BAe)*

Drawing of the throttle controls

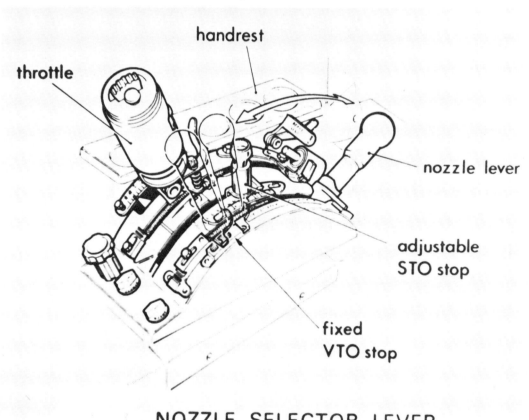

NOZZLE SELECTOR LEVER

This VMA-542 Harrier is in 'hide' at Bogue Field during a 1978 exercise.

A flight of AV-8A Harriers from VMA-513, based at MCAS Yuma, is seen during a 1977 training sortie.   (BAe)

This AV-8A from VMA-231, has new strip lights added to the nose, tail, and on top of outrigger housing. The photo was taken at MCAS Quantico in 1982.

A good front view of an AV-8A from VMA-513 shows two 300-gallon drop tanks, and an Aden gun pod. It was photographed at NAS Alameda on November 6, 1982. *(Chee)*

These AV-8As from VMA-513 are fitted with long range drop tanks at Misawa Air Base, Japan, on August 3, 1975.
(Taylor)

The pilot straps into his AV-8A from VMA-513 during a 1975 Med cruise aboard USS Guam, LPH-5. (USN)

This AV-8A, from VMA-513, is fitted with a refueling probe, at NAS Agana, Guam. It was enroute to MCAS Yuma following a 1980 deployment to Kadena Airfield, Okinawa. (USN)

A Harrier from VMA-231, is shown in hover at MCAS Cherry Point, July 25, 1974.   *(Sullivan)*

A clean AV-8A from VMA-231 was fitted with fuselage strakes in place of gun pods, and was photographed at MCAS Cherry Point in July 1974.   *(Sullivan via Geer)*

This AV-8A of VMAT-203 was painted in the subdued scheme during 1982.

AV-8C

This AV-8C is being towed to the ramp by McAir technicians during flight trials in 1979. The new gun pod strakes are visible in this photo.

The AV-8C designation may seem out of sequence alphabetically, but in actual service terms the AV-8C began squadron duty before the AV-8B. The reason for this is quite simple. During the prototype development for the YAV-8B at NAS Patuxent River, it was discovered lift could be increased by simple mechanical devices attached to the undersides of the fuselage. Previously, increased lift came from upgrading the Pegasus engine. This was considered a costly venture for the limited lift that could be gained with the technology of the time.

But an additional 1,200 lbs. of lift was gained by simple devices called LIDs, an acronym for Lift Improvement Devices. Two modifications comprised the Lift Improvement Devices. Large longitudinal ventral strakes replaced the smaller strakes found on the AV-8A and GR Mk.1 when the Aden gun pods were not attached, or a modified longitudinal ventral strake was added to the gun

pods themselves. Also, a retractable dam or fence was located in front of and between the strakes. This fence falls into position when the landing gear comes down. It traps air under the Harrier during takeoff and landing, using this 'ground effect' to increase lift. A secondary benefit is that this reduces the amount of hot gases reingested by the engine inlets, and thus improves thrust.

This increase in lift was a worthwhile advantage that could easily be applied to the existing AV-8A Harriers with little difficulty, and at the same time give the older AV-8As nearly the same performance as the new AV-8B still in development at Patuxent River. Additional changes included chaff and flare dispensers, rear warning radar (RWR), and an on-board oxygen generating system. As a result, the remaining AV-8As were retrofitted with LIDs, and their designations were changed to AV-8C to coincide with this modification.

The prototype AV-8C is shown here during flight trials at NAS Patuxent River in 1979.

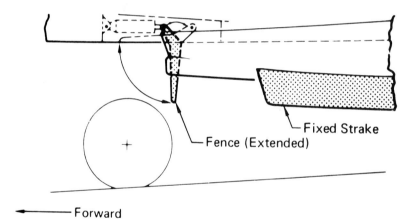

Fixed Strake

Fence (Extended)

Forward

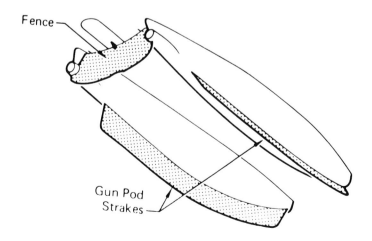

Fence

Gun Pod Strakes

Drawing of Lift Improvement Devices

The prototype AV-8C and No. 1 YAV-8B are seen together during flight deck trials on May 1, 1983. (USN)

An AV-8C Harrier from VMA-542 is painted in the subdued scheme.

AV-8B

The No. 1 YAV-8B is on the McAir ramp at NAS Patuxent River in 1980.

AV-8B (Prototypes & FSD)

Seven years after the first AV-8As entered squadron service with VMA-513 in February 1971, the prototype YAV-8B made its maiden flight at the McDonnell Douglas St. Louis plant on November 9, 1978. McAir test pilot Charles Plummer was in the cockpit for the seven-minute flight, but it was enough to demonstrate the concepts developed for the AV-8B. Basically, the AV-8B embodies the same vectored thrust principles pioneered by Hawker Siddeley, but improves upon this with greater internal fuel capacity and additional ordnance payload. The airframe is similar to the AV-8A at first glance, but upon closer examination a whole new aircraft becomes evident.

The two YAV-8B prototypes, BuNos 158394 (No. 1) and 158395 (No. 2), were the last two AV-8As from the first lot of twelve Harriers delivered to the Marines in 1971. McDonnell Douglas took the two AV-8As to St. Louis for modification and rebuilding to the YAV-8B configuration. The major design change made was the new supercritical wing. This new wing is fourteen percent greater in span than that of the AV-8A, and makes use of new slotted trailing edge flaps. Most significant is the forty percent increase in internal fuel capacity, and raising the number of underwing pylons from four to six. This helped to quiet critics who cried that the Harrier lacked range and payload capability. But the wing itself is the first of its type to be made of composite materials. Graphite and epoxy are used in an all non-metal construction except for the underwing hardpoints. Another noteworthy change is the

revised intake design with a double row of inlet doors. The forward fuselage on the prototypes is the same as the original AV-8A, but production AV-8Bs have a new raised cockpit.

The two prototypes were sent to NAS Patuxent River for additional flight tests and evaluation by Navy and Marine pilots in early 1979, but were returned to St. Louis a year later for additional flight testing. It was at St. Louis where the second prototype, BuNo 158395, was lost during a flight test on November 15, 1979. The result of the crash was due to compressor failure, forcing the McAir test pilot to eject safely. The YAV-8B was a total loss. Nonetheless, the program was considered successful and continued on, resulting in a production order for four Full Scale Development (FSD) AV-8Bs placed in April 1979.

This is the No. 2 YAV-8B prototype shortly before its crash on November 15, 1979.   (McDonnell Douglas)

This YAV-8B is taxiing out for a test hop at NAS Patuxent River.

The differences are easily seen in this photo of an AV-8A and AV-8B during a test flight near St. Louis.

(McDonnell Douglas)

The first of the four Full Scale Development AV-8Bs hovers at St. Louis, and illustrates the new fuselage strakes.
(McDonnell Douglas)

Full Scale Development Program

The first of the new Full Scale Development Harriers, more commonly referred to as FSD, did not make its first flight until November 5, 1981. FSD Harriers No. 2 and No. 3 made their first flights on April 7 and 9, 1982, respectively. The fourth and last FSD Harrier made its first flight more than a year later on June 4, 1983. Eventually all four FSD Harriers were sent to NAS Patuxent River for continuing flight trials, each performing specific tests.

FSD Harrier Test Functions

No. 1, BuNo 161396	Assess general flying qualities
No. 2, BuNo 161397	Measure flight loads, structural integrity, and engine re-light behavior
No. 3, BuNo 161398	Avionics and weapons integration
No. 4, BuNo 161399	GAU-12 25mm Gatling gun test, and production aircraft acceptance criteria

McDonnell Douglas test pilot Bill Lowe steps from the cockpit of the fourth FSD AV-8B following a flight where the Harrier's autopilot took over to make a perfect hands-off vertical landing during December 1982.
(McDonnell Douglas)

FSD Harrier No. 1 is shown here on the ramp at NAS Patuxent River in 1986. It is fitted with four long range drop tanks and two Sidewinder missiles.

The second FSD Harrier was painted glossy white with black. Red areas, trimmed in gold, were for high visibility during spin tests.

(McDonnell Douglas)

FSD Harrier number 2 refuels from a USMC KC-130 tanker near Edwards AFB during the AV-8B's aerial refueling tests in June 1983. *(McDonnell Douglas)*

FSD AV-8B number 2 sits on the McAir ramp at Patuxent River awaiting another test flight in 1982.

The third FSD AV-8B is seen with white edges added to the upper wing surface. The double row of inlet doors around the intakes are visible. A 500-pound Mk-82 practice bomb is attached to the outboard pylon as McAir technicians prepare for its next test flight at Patuxent River. (Brown)

The fourth FSD AV-8B was painted in this two-tone gray low visibility scheme. The colors are light gray, FS 36375, applied to the upper wings, fuselage, and tail surface, with light gray, FS 36495, applied to the center fuselage and remaining areas.

This close-up view shows the double row of inlet doors as first adopted for the YAV-8B and the FSD Harriers.

Here is a good view of the large wing and trailing edge flaps, as well as the LIDs that greatly improve the Harrier's performance. (McDonnell Douglas)

The new raised cockpit and bubble canopy identify this as the new AV-8B Harrier.　　　　　(McDonnell Douglas)

AV-8B (Production)

The FSD testing at NAS Patuxent River was a great success. Even before the program was completed, McDonnell Douglas received an initial production order for twelve AV-8B Harriers which were identified as the pilot production batch. The first of these flew on August 29, 1983. All twelve pilot production AV-8Bs were delivered to the Marines beginning in January 1984.

The production AV-8Bs, as well as the FSD Harriers, differed significantly from the earlier YAV-8B. Foremost, it is a totally new airframe, superficially resembling the original AV-8A, but differing in nearly every way. The cockpit is nothing like that of the AV-8A. It is "state of the art" and very similar to the cockpit of the F/A-18 Hornet. Pilots report it is much easier to fly, and the new bubble canopy has greater all-around visibility. The wing is based on the YAV-8B prototype, and is made of the same composite materials. It has greater fuel capacity and six pylons instead of four, as found on the AV-8A.

The AV-8B has greater range and weapons payload that almost doubles that of the AV-8A, not to mention the increased thrust and lift created by the Lift Improvement Devices. In addition to the LIDs, a new Pegasus 11-21E engine of 23,000 lbs. of thrust (the British designation is Mk.105) has also been added. In addition to the new cockpit, power plant, and larger wing, new Leading-Edge Root extensions, receiving the acronym LERX, have been added to the wing's leading edge where it joins the fuselage. The LERX help improve the Harrier's turning rate

considerably.

AV-8Bs were first delivered to the Harrier training squadron, VMAT-203, at Cherry Point in January 1984. These first AV-8Bs were delivered with a double row of inlet doors surrounding the intakes, a feature first added to the YAV-8B to help improve thrust. However, it was later found that this double row of inlet doors did not work as well as first thought, and they now have been replaced with a single row of inlets as originally produced on the older AV-8As. The first Harriers built with the double row of inlets have all been retrofitted with single row inlet doors.

Current Marine Corps plans seek to establish eight AV-8B attack squadrons of twenty Harriers each, plus the training squadron. In all, 332 AV-8B Harriers have been ordered by the Marines, but the ugly head of politics has entered the picture again. The House Armed Services Committee, under the Chairmanship of Senator Les Aspin, is recommending a reduction in the overall AV-8B force, bringing the total down to 180 Harriers. The Senate, as of this date, has not yet endorsed this recommendation. But the scare is still there. If this recommendation is endorsed by the Senate, and the resulting production cuts become effective, the damage done to the Marine's "posture plans" could be felt into the next century. As one observer put it, "... the irony of it all is that the AV-8B, free of the difficulties that plagued the AV-8A, has progressed with almost no major problems." Hopefully, these cuts will not take place and the AV-8B will serve the Marines as intended.

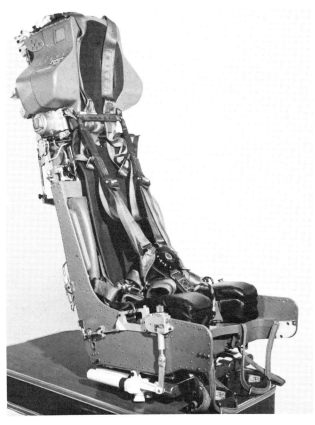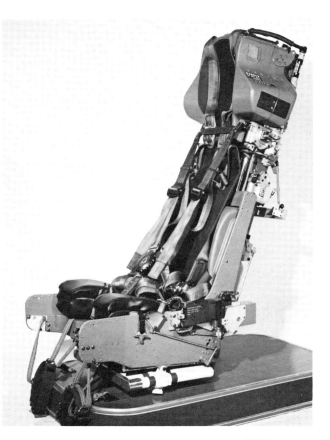

The Stencel type 10B ejection seat is used in the AV-8B.   *(Pilkington)*

The second production AV-8B, that was delivered to the Marines at Cherry Point in 1984, still had the double row of inlet doors, but all were later modified with a single row of doors.

AV-8A COLORS

By the mid-seventies, some color had been added to the markings carried by Marine AV-8As. This Harrier was photographed while serving with VMA-513 at Misawa Air Base on October 3, 1976.   (Spering/AIR)

The WF tail code and white stars on a blue rudder indicate that this AV-8A, 158969, belongs to VMA-513. The photograph was taken at a stop-over at El Paso International Airport in July 1977.   (Kinzey)

This photograph was taken in 1979, and shows the colorful red, white, and blue rudder on an AV-8A from VMAT-203.   (Huston)

AV-8A, 158701, was assigned to VMA-542's Tigers when this photograph was taken in November 1977. (Kinzey)

Perhaps the most colorful of the early AV-8A markings are seen on the Harrier from VMA-231, Det-A, during April 1977.   (Spering/AIR)

The low visibility markings used on the AV-8A are illustrated in this photograph of 159243, which is also assigned to VMA-231. All markings, except for the red and white warning triangles for the ejection seat and the pylons, are black. Note the aircraft number painted on the inside of the speed brake. The photograph was taken in December 1979.   (Spidle)

AV-8A COLOR DETAILS

Right side nose details are shown here. The yaw indicator is mounted on a short mast just ahead of the cockpit. Also note the windshield wiper on the center section of the windscreen. *(Kinzey)*

A combat camera is mounted in the nose, and the lens window is seen here on the left side. Additionally, a camera pod can be carried on the centerline station for the reconnaissance mission. *(Kinzey)*

These two photographs show color details of the landing gear. At left is the nose gear with two lights visible on the strut. The right outrigger gear is seen at right. *(Both Kinzey)*

This is the ventral strake as viewed from the right. Note the red light in the corner. The two other dark areas are antennas. *(Kinzey)*

The open speed brake is seen here from the right. The inside of the brake and the well are painted the same color as the underside of the aircraft. *(Kinzey)*

Details of the instrument panel in the AV-8A are revealed in this photograph. *(Spidle)*

Left console details are visible here. Of particular interest are the throttle quadrant and the control for the exhaust nozzles. *(Spidle)*

This is the right console. *(Spidle)*

The Aden gun pod on the left side is seen here. This photograph was taken before the strakes were added. *(Kinzey)*

This view looks down the left intake to the engine. *(Kinzey)*

The exhaust nozzles on the right side are shown here. Note the two vanes in each nozzle. *(Kinzey)*

AV-8B COCKPIT COLORS

Left view of main instrument panel display.

Right view of main instrument panel.

Left Console with throttle and nozzle selector.

Close-up of control stick.

Right console.

TAV-8B COCKPIT COLORS

Front cockpit instrument panel

Rear cockpit instrument panel.

Front cockpit, right console, with radio and electrical switches

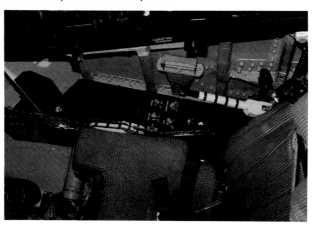

Rear cockpit, right console, with an obvious reduction in electrical switches over that in the front cockpit.

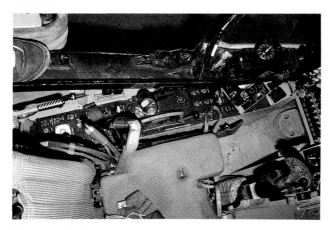

Front cockpit, left console, showing throttle and nozzle controls

Rear cockpit, left console, with throttle and nozzle controls

AV-8B COLORS

The first Harrier squadron to receive the AV-8B was VMAT-203, the Harrier training squadron at MCAS Cherry Point. When first delivered, the AV-8Bs had a double row of inlet doors around the intakes. These were found to be impractical, and the change to the single row of inlet doors can be seen here.

VX-5 still flies a few AV-8Bs for continuing evaluation.
(Sauve)

The first attack squadron to transition from the AV-8A to the AV-8B was VMA-231 in late 1986.

This AV-8B from VMA-331 Bumble Bees is painted in the standard camouflage scheme. Just visible below the windscreen is a painting of a Bumble Bee riding a bomb.

The newest Harrier squadron to form is VMA-223, which transitioned from Skyhawks in late 1987.

The "Gray Ghost" is an AV-8B serving with VMA-331 to evaluate this new low visibility camouflage.

PROTOTYPE & FSD COLORS

The prototype YAV-8B is shown here on the McAir ramp at Patuxent River during June 1978. It was produced by modifying an AV-8A airframe.

The YAV-8C prototype was produced from design advances introduced on the YAV-8B prototype.

The first Full Scale Development AV-8B is seen as it appeared during flight tests at Patuxent River in July 1983.

The second Full Scale Development (FSD) Harrier was painted in this high visibility scheme for easy identification during spin tests.

The all gray No. 4 FSD Harrier carried out armament trials at Patuxent River. It also evaluated this low visibility camouflage scheme.

TWO-SEAT HARRIER COLORS

The TAV-8A Harrier trainer in the photograph at left is shown as it appeared in 1976 with red, white, and blue rudder. By 1982, the colorful tail markings had disappeared and subdued national insignia replaced the red, white, and blue insignia.

Above center: The third production TAV-8B Harrier was delivered to VMAT-203 during January 1988.

Right: A close-up photograph of the TAV-8B's nose section reveals the rear cockpit's windscreen.

DETAIL & SCALE FIVE-VIEW DRAWINGS

DETAIL & SCALE 1/72nd SCALE

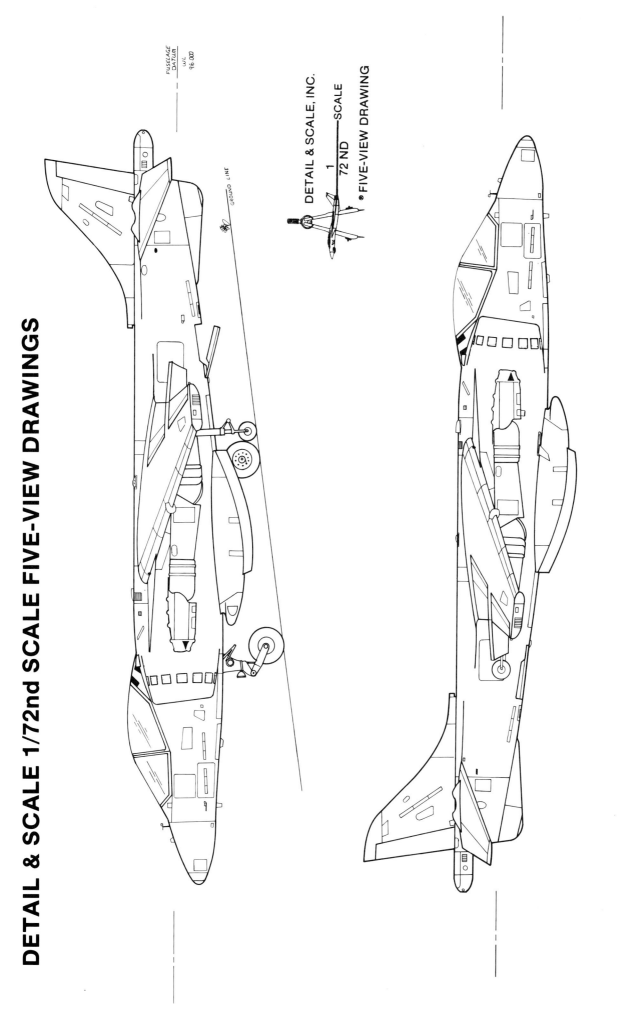

FUSELAGE
DATUM
W.L
96.000

GROUND LINE

DETAIL & SCALE, INC.

1
————— SCALE
72 ND

⊛ FIVE-VIEW DRAWING

Dana Bell

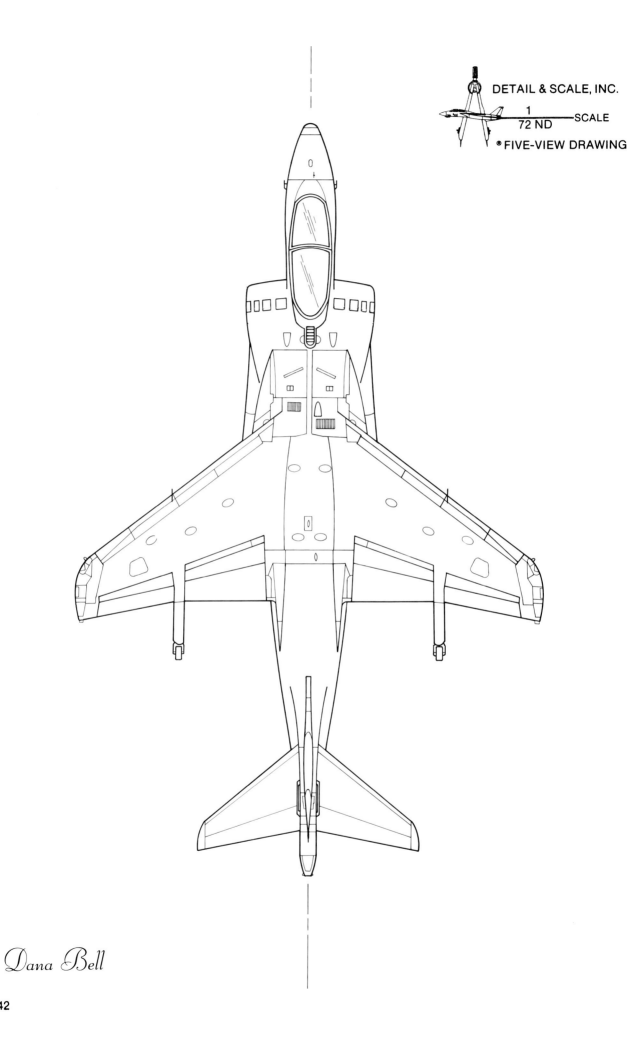

Dana Bell

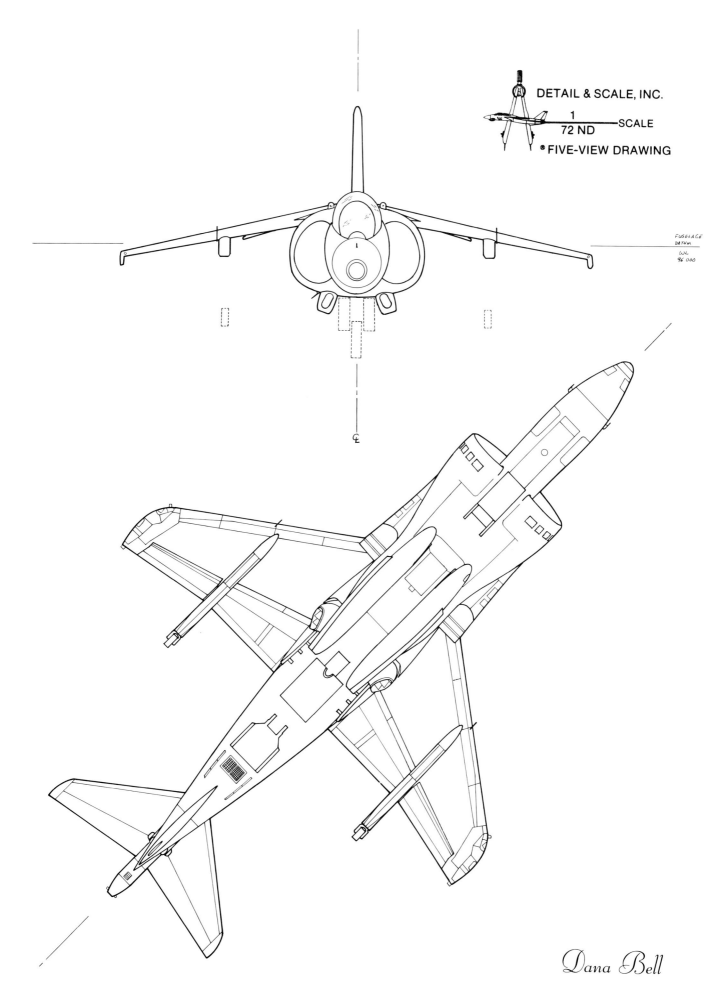

DETAIL & SCALE, INC.

$\dfrac{1}{72\text{ ND}}$ —SCALE

® FIVE-VIEW DRAWING

FUSELAGE
DATUM
WL
96 000

Dana Bell

This close-up photograph provides a view of an AV-8B refueling from a KC-10 tanker in 1987. *(Spering/AIR)*

During the transition to AV-8Bs in 1984, the CO of VMAT-203 was Col. M.D. Ryan. *(Spering/AIR)*

AV-8B Flying Characteristics

As previously stated, pilots report the new AV-8B to be easier to fly than the AV-8A. Col. M.D. Ryan, Commanding Officer of VMAT-203 when the first AV-8Bs were delivered in January 1984, explains the differences, "From a squadron point of view, we expect to get a lot out of the AV-8B over the AV-8A, and even the A-4. Listed in order, we have greater safety and ease of flying, greater range and payload, and improved navigation systems and bombing accuracy. On the maintenance side, the reliability and maintainability is expected to be considerably improved, although reliability and maintainability cannot be judged over this short period of time since they are new airplanes."

Responding to a question regarding the results of the Lift Improvement Devices, Col. Ryan added, "The LIDs are stated to add 1,200 lbs. of thrust, depending on the regime of operations. In the vertical regime the 1,200 lbs. of thrust is pretty close. But in the short takeoff regime, because of the huge wing and flaps, the advantages are dramatic!"

"But when we talk about payload and range," Col.

A clean AV-8B from VMAT-203 is shown here during a spring 1987 training flight.   *(Spering/AIR)*

Ryan continues, "the AV-8A was typically taking off with drop tanks which gave 6,800 lbs. of gas, total. Without drop tanks, the AV-8B has an additional 900 lbs. of fuel over the AV-8A. So without taking up those two stations with drop tanks, you now have seven pylons for weapons. On the AV-8A, because of the need to carry drop tanks, there are only three pylons for weapons."

Discussing the advantages of the AV-8B with its larger wing and increased internal fuel capacity, Col. Ryan said, "Typically, we take off with an AV-8A with two drop tanks, still having less fuel and endurance than the AV-8B with internal fuel only. Takeoff speed for a short takeoff in the AV-8A would be about 95 knots. The AV-8B's takeoff speed would be about 65 knots! This means the AV-8B has increased payload by 1,000 lbs., and increased gross weight of the airplane taking off by 2,000 lbs. At the same time the takeoff speed is reduced by about thirty percent! This is primarily due to the big flaps and bigger wing. It is a dramatic improvement." Continuing, Col. Ryan adds, "In short takeoff performance you gain about 1,000 to 1,200 lbs. of thrust. In vertical takeoff capability that is not a significant gain. Operationally you do not want to do vertical takeoffs because it requires more fuel and therefore less payload. Operationally you want short takeoffs, because you can carry much more."

Reviewing the AV-8B cockpit and comparing it with the AV-8A, VMAT-203's CO adds, "The thing to remember is the AV-8B cockpit reflects a completely different way of training our pilots because this is a sys-

tems airplane, and it is easy to fly V/STOL. I'm convinced I could probably take an AV-8A pilot and give him no schooling on the airplane, except how to start it, and he could fly the AV-8B safely. On the other side of the coin, the AV-8A is not a systems oriented airplane. It's strictly VFR with a manual bombing system and a manual navigation--taking out the map just like in World War II, flying by time, distance and pilotage. The bombing in the AV-8A requires the pilot to achieve a predetermined dive angle, a predetermined air speed, a predetermined release altitude with pipper on predetermined aim point. That's all up to the pilot. In the AV-8B this is all done by computers. We're finding the biggest problem is how to manage the system, both navigation and attack mode. Once a pilot learns the systems, and it doesn't take long to learn, he becomes much more effective. So far the accuracy of the navigation system has been extremely good. We are routinely coming back to base after an hour and fifteen minute flight, or longer, with less than one mile inaccuracy, that's if you don't do any updates in the air!"

When asked about the AV-8B HUD, Ryan responded, "Most AV-8A pilots have to bend over to see through the information displayed on their HUD. The information is rudimentary; altitude, air speed, and heading. The AV-8B has everything you could ask for, very similar to that in the F/A-18; engine RPM, nozzle angle, flap angle, engine JPT, velocity vector in V/STOL mode, and of course heading, air speed, and altitude as always. You can basically fly the HUD without looking down provided the

The newest Harrier squadron to form is VMA-223, which transitioned from Skyhawks in late 1987.

system is properly programmed for the mission. If you want to change the weapons you are planning on releasing, or how you want to release them, or change navigation points, then you have to look down into the cockpit multipurpose display to 'call up' and change information. But if the navigation systems and weapons systems are programmed properly for the mission, you could fly the whole mission without looking down. We don't do that because it doesn't take that long to look down, but it is nice to know that when you get down to low altitude at high speeds, you don't have to look inside the cockpit to accomplish the mission, everything is displayed in the HUD!''

An AV-8B Harrier from VMA-331 is pictured during the squadron's first carrier quals in June 1985.

(GYSGT Brown, USMC)

The Ace of Spades on the nose of this VMA-231 AV-8B is barely visible on the subdued wrap-around camouflage scheme. *(Brown)*

AV-8B Specifications

Prime Contractor	McDonnell Aircraft Company, division of McDonnell Douglas
Type	Single seat, advanced light attack V/STOL jet aircraft
Planned USMC Program	332 aircraft
Powerplant	Rolls Royce Pegasus 11-21E thrust vectoring turbofan, rated at 21,450 lbs. of thrust
Length	46 feet, 4 inches
Height	11 feet, 8 inches
Wingspan	30 feet, 4 inches, 230 square feet
Max speed (sea level)	580 knots, Mach .88
Range	1,720 nautical miles with four 300-gallon drop tanks

This photo of the upper surfaces of an AV-8B with its refueling probe extended was taken following refueling from a KC-10 tanker. *(Spering/AIR)*

The third AV-8B squadron to form was VMA-542, based at MCAS Cherry Point. (Becker)

This VMA-331 Bumble Bees AV-8B has drop tanks and AIM-9 launch rails installed.

The "Gray Ghost" AV-8B is assigned to VMA-331 to evaluate this low visibility camouflage, slightly different from the gray scheme of FSD Harrier No. 4.

AV-8B COCKPIT LAYOUT

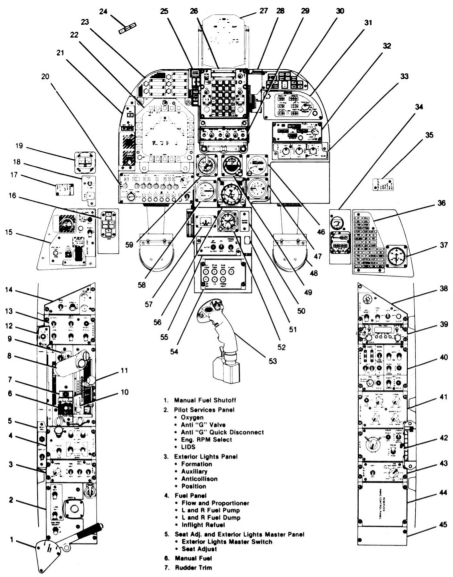

1. Manual Fuel Shutoff
2. Pilot Services Panel
   • Oxygen
   • Anti "G" Valve
   • Anti "G" Quick Disconnect
   • Eng. RPM Select
   • LIDS
3. Exterior Lights Panel
   • Formation
   • Auxiliary
   • Anticollison
   • Position
4. Fuel Panel
   • Flow and Proportioner
   • L and R Fuel Pump
   • L and R Fuel Dump
   • Inflight Refuel
5. Seat Adj. and Exterior Lights Master Panel
   • Exterior Lights Master Switch
   • Seat Adjust
6. Manual Fuel
7. Rudder Trim

8. Throttle
   • Flaps
   • Slew Control/Designator
   • Air Start
   • Cage/Uncage
   • Finger Lift
   • Communication No. 1, No. 2 and Both
   • Speed Brake
9. Jet Pipe Temperature Limiter
10. Nozzle Control Stop
11. Nozzle Position Control
12. ECM Initiate
13. Stability Augmentation/Attitude Hold Panel
   • AFC On/Reset
   • Alt Hold
   • Yaw
   • Pitch
   • Roll
   • Q Feel
14. Trim Position Panel
   • Rudder Trim Indicator
   • Aileron Trim Indicator
   • Approach Light
   • Rudder Pedal Shaker Test/On/Off
15. Landing Gear and Flap Panel
   • Landing Gear Selector
   • Antiskid/Nose Wheel Steering
   • Flap Cruise/STOL
   • Flap Position Indicator
   • Flap On/Off/Reset
   • Down Lock Override
   • BIT
   • Emergency Jettison
16. Landing Gear Position Lights
17. Landing Checklist

18. Water and Combat Select Panel
   • Water On/Off/Dump
   • Combat Select
19. Standby Compass
20. Armament Control Panel (ACP)
21. Master Arm Panel
   • Master Arm
   • Mode Select
     — Navigation
     — Air/Ground
     — V/STOL
   • Flare Slave
22. Multipurpose Display (MPD)
23. Options Display Unit (ODU)
24. Inflight Refueling Lights
25. Priority Caution Lights
   • Master Caution
   • R and L Fuel Low
   • Hydraulics
   • Bingo
   • Water
   • 15 Sec
26. Integrated Control Panel (ICP)
27. Head-Up Display (HUD)
28. HUD Camera
29. HUD Control Panel
30. Warning and Threat Lights
31. Engine Display Panel (EDP)
   • Stabilator Position
   • Nozzle Position
   • Tachometer
   • Jet Pipe Temperature
   • Fuel Flow
   • BIT
   • Duct Pressure
   • Water Quantity
   • Water Flow Light

32. Fuel Quantity Indicator Panel
   • Fuel Quantity Indicators
   • Bingo Fuel Set
   • Indicator Select
33. ECM Panel
   • Radar Warning Receiver
   • Expendables
   • Defensive Electronic Countermeasures
34. Brake and Hydraulic Pressure Indicators
   • Brake Pressure
   • Hydraulic Pressure System No. 1 and No. 2
35. Takeoff Check List
36. Caution and Advisory Lights
37. Cabin Pressure Altitude Indicator
38. Electrical Panel
   • Battery State of Charge Indicator
   • Battery
   • Generator
   • Engine Start
   • APU
39. Radio Remote Control Unit
40. Auxiliary CNI Panel (ACNIP)
41. Interior Lights Panel
   • Console Lights
   • Instrument Panel Lights
   • Flood Lights
   • Compass Light/Lights Test
   • Warning/Caution
42. Environment Control System Panel
   • Temperature Controller
   • Cabin Pressure/Dump
   • Defog
43. Sensor Panel
   • Dual Mode Tracker
   • Inertial Navigation System Selector

44. Blank Panel (Reserved AMAC)
45. Blank Panel
46. Altimeter
47. Vertical Speed Indicator
48. Rudder Pedal
49. Attitude Indicator
50. Radio Call Number (Bureau Number)
51. Rudder Pedal Adjust
52. Clock
53. Stick Grip
   • Air/Ground Weapon Release
   • Trim Button
   • Sensor Select
     — HUD Select (FWD)
     — Dual Mode Tracker Select (Aft)
       — Laser Search Track (1)
       — TV Search Track (2)
   • Air-to-Air Weapon Select
     — Sidewinder (FWD)
     — SEAM (Aft)
     — Gun (Depress)
   • Nose Wheel Steer/Undesignate
   • SAAHS Disengage
   • Gun/Sidewinder
54. Circuit Breaker Panel
55. Miscellaneous Switch Panel
   • Display Processor
   • Mission Computer
   • Probe Heat
56. Horizontal Situation Indicator
57. Turn and Slip Indicator
58. Angle-of-Attack Indicator
59. Airspeed Indicator

See page 36 for photographs of the AV-8B cockpit.

WEAPONS & STORES

Weapons carried by the AV-8B are seen in this publicity photograph.　　　　　*(McDonnell Douglas)*

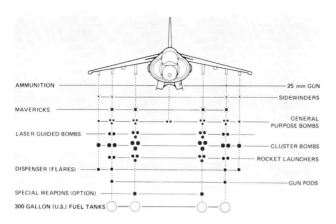

AMMUNITION	25 mm GUN
	SIDEWINDERS
MAVERICKS	
	GENERAL PURPOSE BOMBS
LASER GUIDED BOMBS	
	CLUSTER BOMBS
	ROCKET LAUNCHERS
DISPENSER (FLARES)	
	GUN PODS
SPECIAL WEAPONS (OPTION)	
300 GALLON (U.S.) FUEL TANKS	

**CLOSE AIR SUPPORT
MISSION**

16 MK-82s	9,120 LB
FUEL	5,114 LB
T.O. WEIGHT	28,350 LB
RADIUS	158 NM

Mission profiles

INTERDICTION MISSION

7 MK-82s	3,990 LB
FUEL	
INTERNAL	7,500 LB
EXTERNAL	2,752 LB
T.O. WEIGHT	28,350 LB
RADIUS	601 NM

At first glance it may appear that the AV-8B carries two gun pods just like the AV-8A did. This is not the case. In fact, the AV-8B carries one 25mm gun that can be attached to the underside of the fuselage. The gun itself is housed in the pod on the left side that is seen here. The muzzle opening is visible at the front end of the pod.

The right side of the pod contains the ammunition for the 25mm gun.

Two long range drop tanks and a Sidewinder missile are loaded on this Harrier.

The TACS pod electronically feeds back information on air combat sorties over the Tactical Air Combat Range to a receiver on the ground, and helps accurately score air combat events.

500-pound bomb fixed to AV-8B's inboard pylon

Three Napalm bombs are fitted to this AV-8B.

DETAILS

The heart of the AV-8B Harrier is the Rolls Royce Pegasus-404 engine. (McDonnell Douglas)

Above: Close-up of original AV-8B cockpit area

Right: Detail view of the AV-8B revised inlet doors

The right front nozzle is shown here from the front.

This is the right rear nozzle from behind.

These two views show the tail cone.

Top left and right: Left and right flare dispensers

Retractable cockpit step

Refueling probe detail

The LID fence and its recess are shown in this close-up photo.

This is the ventral fuselage strake on the right side. It is used when the gun is not carried.

The open speed brake is seen here from the right.

WING DETAILS

Upper wing surface details are revealed in these two photos.

This is the wingtip detail on the right wing.

This photograph shows the right Leading Edge Root Extension (LERX) and the fire access hole.

LANDING GEAR DETAILS

The nose gear is seen from the front right in this photograph.

Details of the nose wheel can be seen here.

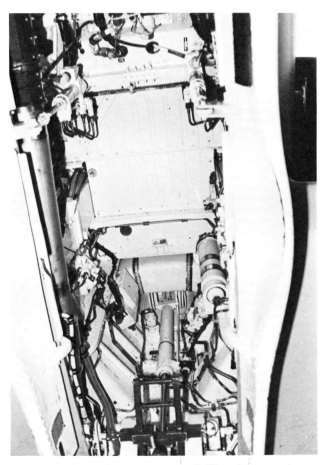

This view shows the nose gear well. The photograph was taken looking up and slightly aft.

Left: This view shows the AV-8A's rear main landing gear as seen from behind and slightly to the right.

Bottom left: The right outrigger gear is shown here.

The long, narrow well for the right outrigger gear is seen in this photo that looks up and forward.

The first AV-8B equipped for night attack missions made its first flight during June 1986.   (McDonnell Douglas)

NIGHT ATTACK HARRIER

Col. Ryan is justifiably proud of the new AV-8B Harriers, but new developments are taking place to improve upon what is already considered a good thing. McDonnell Douglas has begun work on developing a new night attack version of the AV-8B. The new night attack AV-8B (BuNo 162966) made its first flight on June 26, 1987, at McAir's St. Louis facility. The Night Attack Harrier features a forward-looking infrared sensor located in a housing on the upper nose area near the yaw indicator, and color digital moving map. The pilot will also wear special night vision goggles.

This new system will be fitted to all AV-8B Harriers beginning in 1989 if funding is approved. This new capability will enhance the Harrier's ability to provide around-the-clock air support for ground troops. "We've expanded the hours of the day that the Marine pilots will be able to employ the weapons systems," said AV-8B general manager and vice president Ed Harper. Harper said the AV-8B night attack program is being developed in cooperation with the McDonnell Douglas F/A-18 Hornet fighter program for the Marine Corps and the US Navy.

The key to the new nighttime capability is a forward looking infrared sensor that 'sees' in the dark. Located in the nose of the Harrier, this sensor provides the pilot with a video picture of the scene ahead of the aircraft on a wide field of view, head-up display.

A multipurpose color display in the cockpit, made by Smith's Industries, Ltd., provides the pilot with a color digital moving map. It gives a video picture of the charts and maps used for mission planning and execution. The map, designed and built by the Sperry Corporation, displays navigational data and important threat intelligence information. The navigational data is stored on a laser disk.

The controls for the forward-looking infrared sensor and digital moving map are located on the flight stick as part of the AV-8B's hands-on-throttle-and-stick operation.

But again, funding from Congress will be the deciding factor on the implementation of this worthwhile and important new system.

TWO-SEAT HARRIERS

This head-on photograph of a TAV-8A was taken during refueling from a KC-10 tanker.

TAV-8A

The two-seat Harrier entered service with the US Marines in the summer of 1976, and became operational with VMAT-203 that August. A total of eight TAV-8As were ordered in Fiscal Year 1973. The TAV-8A is similar to the RAF's T Mk.4 two-seat Harrier trainer. But the Marine's TAV-8A was also developed to perform a secondary role of Tactical Airborne Controller.

Because of its secondary role of Tactical Airborne Controller, the Marine's TAV-8As not only have a complete rear cockpit for instructor/student training, but there is also a full range of Tactical VHF and UHF radios for the airborne commander to operationally control his single-seat AV-8As, or to talk to Marine ground forces.

The TAV-8As completed successful ship-board operational trials in late 1976 aboard USS Franklin D. Roosevelt (CVA-42). The eight two-seat Harriers were allotted the BuNos 159563-159569.

Upper surface detail of a TAV-8A   *(Spering/AIR)*

VMAT-203 is the only USMC squadron equipped with TAV-8As like this one seen landing at NAS Oceana in 1983.

This TAV-8A was photographed during a cross-country training flight from MCAS Cherry Point to NAS Fallon, Nevada, in March 1987. The refueling probe on the TAV-8A is longer than those on the AV-8A due to the lengthened cockpit.

Both student and instructor pilots in this TAV-8A prepare to take off for a training flight on March 11, 1987.

This 1976 photo illustrates the colorful rudders painted on Harriers during that period. (Sullivan)

TAV-8A DETAILS

Close-up of an open TAV-8A cockpit

Cockpit area and inlet door details during engine run-up

Open canopy detail

Yaw indicators for front and rear cockpits

Rear cockpit windscreen on a TAV-8A

Above: TAV-8A speed brake detail

Right: Inlet door details

Below left and right: Left and right side views of the TAV-8A tailcone

TAV-8B

The prototype TAV-8B is seen here during its first flight in November 1986.   (McDonnell Douglas)

The first TAV-8B made its first flight on October 21, 1986. "The first flight went about as well as any first flight could," said Bill Lowe, chief experimental test pilot at McDonnell Douglas. "While the flight envelope was limited," Lowe added, "within those limits it handled very much like its single-seat counterpart, the AV-8B."

This new two-seat Harrier will replace the original Hawker Siddeley TAV-8As still serving with VMAT-203. And just as the TAV-8A was developed from the single-seat AV-8A, or more correctly the RAF's GR Mk.1, the new TAV-8B was developed from the new McDonnell Douglas AV-8B. "The TAV-8B will be almost identical to the single-seat AV-8B in handling qualities, cockpit arrangements, avionics displays and armament," said vice president Ed Harper.

The new TAV-8B will have the same advantages over the TAV-8A as the AV-8B has over the AV-8A, with a substantial increase in payload and range, and it has likewise been developed to include the secondary role of Airborne Tactical Controller.

The physical differences in the new trainer versus the AV-8B include a lengthened forward fuselage to accommodate the second cockpit, a seventeen-inch taller vertical tail to give added directional stability, dual flight and engine controls, and a modified environmental control system.

The front cockpit seat for the student pilot is the same as in the AV-8B. The instructor pilot has duplicate controls and excellent visibility from the rear cockpit's elevated seat. The TAV-8B is also capable of carrying as many as six Mk-76 practice bombs, four LAU-68 rocket launchers, or two 300-gallon drop tanks on two wing stations for tactical weapons training.

This first of twenty-eight TAV-8B Harrier trainers went first to NAS Patuxent River during the spring of 1987 for operational flight testing, and finally to MCAS Cherry Point in June of 1987 to begin squadron service.

TAV-8B Specifications

Prime Contractor	McDonnell Aircraft Company, division of McDonnell Douglas
Type	Two-seat V/STOL trainer
Planned USMC Program	28
Powerplant	Rolls Royce Pegasus 11-21E thrust vectoring turbofan rated at 21,450 lbs. of thrust
Length	46 feet, 4 inches
Height	13 feet, 5 inches
Wingspan	30 feet, 4 inches, 230 square feet
Max Speed (sea level)	580 knots, Mach .88
External Stores	Two stores stations capable of carrying six Mk-76 practice bombs, four LAU-68 rocket launchers, or two external fuel tanks.

The first production TAV-8B made its first flight in July 1987. The Marines plan to buy twenty-eight new TAV-8Bs. *(McDonnell Douglas)*

This is a close-up of the cockpit area of the new TAV-8B prototype.

The first three TAV-8B two-seat Harrier trainers were assigned to VMAT-203 at Cherry Point during January 1988.

MODELERS SECTION

KIT REVIEWS

Notes:

Most kits of the Harrier that have been released are still generally available. Those that are have been reviewed below by members of the Delaware Valley (Philadelphia) Chapter of IPMS/USA. The kits that are no longer on the market are also included. A summary or comments on them are made by Jim Galloway, who is a well known kit collector in IPMS and modeling circles. While his comments are not full reviews of these kits, they do provide useful information to the collector as well as the modeler who might have one of these kits sitting on the shelf from years past.

Since this book deals only with USMC Harriers, only those kits that can be built as one of the versions flown by the Marines are included in this modelers section. Other kits will be reviewed in the future volume that will cover foreign Harriers.

1/200th SCALE KIT

Playkit Harrier, Kit Number 50422
Comments by Jim Galloway

Although this model was released in 1984, it is already considered a collector's item, and it is no longer generally available. It falls more into the toy category, and is a poor representation of the Harrier. It would not appeal to the serious modeler, and would interest only the die-hard collector. It was a snap-together type of kit, and consisted of eleven pieces molded in dark gray plastic. Instead of decals, it had stickers for one **U.S. AIR FORCE** and two number **3**s. Its present market value even to a collector is only about $1.00.

1/144th SCALE KITS

Crown AV-8A/GR Mk.1/GR Mk.3, Kit Number P831
Comments by Jim Galloway

Thirty-nine pieces of gray plastic and a clear canopy make up this small kit of the Harrier. There are alternate parts for a gear down or an in-flight gear up model. Decals are provided for an AV-8A of VMA-513, and include national insignias, a **WF** tail code, and a BuNo of 158387. The cockpit has a seat, but there is no other detail provided. It was also released as only a GR Mk.3 with British markings as kit number P822. While this kit is not considered a collector's item, it may take some searching to find one.

Revell AV-8 Harrier, Kit Number 1045
Comments by Jim Galloway

This is a re-release by Revell of the Crown kit number P831 listed above. It was issued as part of their "Squadron 144" series. The decal sheet has only one **WF** tail code and one **MARINES**. British markings are also provided.

1/100th SCALE KIT

Takara AV-8A/GR Mk.3, Kit Number 441005
Comments by Jim Galloway

Issued in 1984, this is the only kit of the Harrier available in 1/100th scale. It is well detailed with very fine engraved panel lines. Optional nose pieces are provided for the standard and "thimble nose." Optional landing gear pieces allow the modeler to build the kit in the gear down or in-flight configurations. A heavy ordnance load consists of nine bombs, four rocket pods, one napalm bomb, two fuel tanks, and two cannon pods. The cockpit has only a seat, so other detailing must be added. There is no seated pilot for the model if it is built with the gear up to represent the aircraft in flight. Two figures are provided for a diorama, and part of the inside of the box is printed with a section of alert pad that can be used as a base. Decals include a Marine AV-8A, 159242, with a tail code of **NM.** It is from VMA-231.

1/72nd SCALE KITS

Airfix Harrier, Kit Number 266
Review and model by Reggie Rogers

This kit represents an early Harrier GR Mk.1. It is one of Airfix's earlier efforts, and this shows in the engineering. The shape of the fuselage is suspect both in plan and elevation according to published references. The wings are devoid of any vortex generators which are a feature on the real aircraft. The main landing gear and outriggers do not align properly, giving a cocked sit to the finished model. I tried to shorten the nose gear and flatten the tires, but had no luck.

Decals are provided for one RAF Harrier only, and no USMC markings are included. The painting guide refers to Airfix's own brand of paint by number. The kit's ninety parts are molded in a light gray plastic with some slight warpage and flash. The canopy is one piece and slightly thick, but it has no mold marks. The wings and fuselage halves fit together properly, but some of the panel lines

The 1/72nd scale Airfix Harrier is an old kit and shows its age.

don't always match.

The surface detail is nicely done in raised panel lines even if they don't all match. The tail surfaces look good, but the gear doors and the speed brake leave a lot to be desired. Some filling is required for a smooth finish. This kit does have a nice selection of weapons, Matra pods, large drop tanks, small drop tanks, Aden gun pods, and a recce pod. For its day this was not a bad kit, but if you are a serious Harrier modeler, this is not the kit to use.

ESCI AV-8A, Kit Number 9051
Review and model by Walter G. Weich

This is a worthwhile Harrier kit, with few major problem areas. The seventy-four pieces are crisply molded with no flash. They fit together well, except for the wing. The canopy is molded in two pieces and includes a HUD. A neat feature is the windshield wiper and housing molded into the windscreen.

Surface detail looks good with neatly scribed panel lines, including the inlet doors surrounding the intakes.

The 1/72nd scale ESCI Harrier is a good kit, but needs some work at the wing-to-fuselage fit.

Other extra details include the dive brake molded separately to allow you to model the dive brake open or closed. Additionally, the VHF antenna and yaw indicator are also molded as separate pieces.

The cockpit is well done with side consoles and a decent Stencel ejection seat. Decals for the instrument panel and side consoles are included.

The major problem area is the wing-to-fuselage fit. The two areas do not match up properly, and will require some work to get a good fit. Further, the wing dihedral seems off, almost looking too flat. As a result, the outrigger wheels do not sit flat.

Two sets of decals are included, one for a Spanish Matador, and the other for an AV-8A of VMA-542. Weapons include two Aden gun pods and two undetermined Sidewinder missiles. Two drop tanks are also included.

In summing up, this is not a bad kit, although it does need a little work with the wings. The finished model is a good replica of the real thing.

Fujimi AV-8A, Kit Number 7A-B3
Review and model by Ralph Ratcliffe

Fujimi has elected to make three different Harrier kits; the AV-8A/GR Mk.1, GR Mk.3, and the Sea Harrier, each

This is the Fujimi 1/72nd scale AV-8A.

having a common center fuselage section, wings, and landing gear. Nose, tail, and canopy parts make up the major differences for each kit. With this comes a lot of joining together of parts to build the model Harrier you desire. This causes a few problems in assembly, especially in the nose-to-center fuselage joint. The intakes also do not fit correctly, and there is a gap in the undersides of the wing.

The quality of the molded parts is good, with very nicely scribed panel lines. Landing gear detail is fair, but with absolutely no detail inside the wheel wells. The cockpit detail is sparse, and has an ejection seat that looks close to the Stencel seat in the AV-8A. The one-piece canopy is crisply molded, but doesn't fit well to the finished model. The speed brake is molded separately, as is a very neat refueling probe.

Weapons are ample and include two 1000-pound bombs, two rocket pods, two Mk-82 500-pound bombs, two NATO cluster bombs, two AIM-9J Sidewinders, two Aden gun pods, and two 100-gallon drop tanks. Decals for two different squadrons in the subdued black style are included for VMA-231 and VMA-542.

With some work on the nose-to-center fuselage joint, and extra detailing in the cockpit, this kit can be made into a fairly good looking model of the Harrier.

Hasegawa Hawker Siddeley Harrier, Kit No. 028
Review and model by Marin F. Ennis

This kit is molded in seventy pieces with a one-piece canopy. There was some flash on the smaller parts, and the canopy had a few scratches, but overall, the parts look good.

The fit of the kit is generally good except for a few problem areas. The worst is where the wing joins the fuselage. This required some filling and sanding. Another annoying area was the tail piece and fuselage joint which also required some filling in. The canopy fit to the fuselage was also poor.

The panel lines are raised and look correct, but the vortex generators on the wings look too heavy and out of scale. Rivet detail should be eliminated since they would be about the size of softballs on the real thing.

Cockpit detail is virtually nil. It is comprised of a seat, instrument panel, and instrument panel decal. The same

The 1/72nd scale Hasegawa AV-8A is not one of their better kits.

The 1/72nd scale Italeri AV-8B was also released by Testors. It is basically a good kit.

holds true for the wheel well detail, only in this case there's nothing there.

When building any Harrier kit, special care should be taken in mating the wings to the fuselage in order for the model to sit properly on the outrigger wheels. I recommend using tube glue for this step since this allows for adjustments before drying. The kit is also inaccurate in building the USMC version due to the lack of any VHF antenna either in the kit or on the box art. The VHF antenna is easily made from sheet plastic. Also, new gun ports should be added to the Aden gun pods.

Decals are of good quality and represent two RAF Harriers and one USMC Harrier from VMA-513. They adhere well and only require a small amount of Solvaset.

Basically, this kit isn't all that bad. The fit is generally good, and the selection of markings is also good. The kit is enhanced by a respectable ordnance selection. It is a good starter kit for the initial venture in building a Harrier, but for a builder with a few models under his belt, this kit offers possibilities for a lesson in how to convert a mediocre kit to a level of reasonable accuracy. On a scale of one to ten, it's a six, and that's with charitable scoring.

Italeri/Testors AV-8B/GR.5, Kit Number 688
Review and model by Reggie Rogers

This kit is typically Italeri. It is very good with a few glitches. The kit contains seventy-four pieces with a small amount of flash and very slight warpage of some parts. The canopy is molded in two pieces and is crisp with no mold marks. Some putty is needed in the wing root area and at the intakes.

Painting the finished model was difficult due to masking the nozzles. But when this kit was first released, the AV-8B was camouflaged much like the AV-8A with light gray undersides. The new production Harriers have a wrap-around scheme that should make painting the model a bit easier. The cockpit interior is nicely detailed, but cries out for some additional detailing because of its visibility under the open bubble canopy. The surface

detail is represented by raised panel lines, and the double row of inlet doors is represented by scribed lines. This feature has been changed on the newer AV-8Bs to a single row of inlet doors, and should not be a problem to change. But then this also allows you to build any of the prototypes, or do a few minor changes to model a production AV-8B.

The stores are the worst feature in the kit, consisting of six Mk-82 Snakeye bombs with TERS and two AIM-9 Sidewinder missiles. Some of the bombs were warped and the fins broken away. The wing is very nicely done and captures the real thing. It includes separate LERX parts, again allowing you to model the prototypes without LERXs, or the production AV-8B with LERXs. But the flap area has a few sink marks that need to be filled in and sanded smooth.

Decals in my kit are off register, but the colors are correct and featured markings for prototypes #1 and #3, and RAF roundels for a GR Mk.5. All in all, this is a very nice kit.

Lindberg Harrier, Kit Number 980
Comments by Jim Galloway

This is probably the worst of the 1/72nd scale Harrier kits, and is of poor quality throughout. It consists of twenty-nine parts molded in green plastic, a blue stand, and a clear canopy. It is a kid's kit only, and the decals are for a British aircraft coded **027**. No USMC markings are included.

Matchbox/AMT AV-8A/GR.1, Kit Number PK-16
Review and model by Walter G. Weich

This is Matchbox's first Harrier kit, and it was later retooled to produce the Sea Harrier after the Falklands Conflict. The kit comprises fifty-six pieces molded in two colors, and a one-piece canopy. The canopy is clear with no mold marks, but appears to be too flat.

The fit of the kit is generally good with no real problem areas. But the infamous Matchbox deep panel lines are

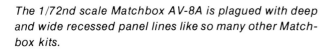

The 1/72nd scale Matchbox AV-8A is plagued with deep and wide recessed panel lines like so many other Matchbox kits.

The 1/48th scale Tamiya AV-8A is shown here.

present. The cockpit is very sparse, but has plenty of room for extra detailing. The inside of the intakes look too narrow, especially when compared to the outside. All of the inlet doors are molded in the open position, an unusual feature, but it allows the modeler to detail the doors properly. Two rocket pods are the only weapons included. Fuselage strakes are provided in place of Aden gun pods. The gear doors are molded closed with no panel lines to represent the doors.

Decals for an RAF GR Mk.1 of No. 3 squadron and an AV-8A of the Marine's VMA-513 appear accurate and well done. Except for the deep panel lines, this is not a bad kit if you consider the release date.

1/48th SCALE KITS

Tamiya Hawker Siddeley Harrier, Kit Number MA112
Review and model by George R. Waeckel, Jr.

This kit is molded in 111 pieces of gray plastic with a crisp two-piece canopy. It is free of flash, although some sink marks were found on the outrigger fairings. Raised panel lines make up the surface detail, and the vortex generators molded on the wings are oversized. The instruction sheet is clear and easy to follow.

The overall fit of this kit can be rated as good to excellent with two exceptions. The most obvious problem area is the fit of the engine access door on top of the center fuselage. This is molded separately to show off the Pegasus engine included in the kit, but it is difficult to blend in the resulting seam if you decide to display your model with the access door closed. The other problem area is the two-piece construction of the nozzles. This seam is also difficult to hide.

The cockpit is adequate with an ejection seat, instrument panel, and side consoles, although we were uncertain as to which type this ejection seat was intended to be. The inlet doors were molded closed, which is rather surprising for a kit in this scale. The Aden gun pods are not

shaped properly, are missing some of the prominent bulges, and there were no muzzle openings.

Decals offer markings for two RAF Harriers, one Spanish Matador, and an AV-8A of VMA-513. Weapons and external stores, other than the previously mentioned Aden guns, include five 1000-pound bombs, four rocket pods, two 100-gallon drop tanks, and a reconnaissance pod.

Monogram Hawker Harrier, Kit Number 5420
Review and model by Paul Florence

This kit contains seventy-five parts molded in dark gray plastic with a two-piece canopy. Typical Monogram quality of raised panel lines is used to represent surface detail. The overall quality of the parts looks good with plenty of extra detail molded in. The exhaust grills on the upper wing and the wheel well detailing are two good examples.

The cockpit area is nicely done with the floor, side consoles, and rear bulkhead molded in one piece. The side consoles have instrument and switch details molded in, as does the separate instrument panel. The ejection seat is a good representation of the Stencel seat found in the AV-8A. Continuing with the cockpit area, the canopy is crisp and clear, and comes with a separate canopy rail. However, the windscreen was slightly warped.

The problem area is getting the outrigger wheels to sit properly. It appears that the main landing gear is too long, but flattening the tires helps to get the correct sit. There is a gap in the fit of the lower wing sections, where they mate to the fuselage, that requires some work.

The intakes look good with the correct number of inlet doors left open. Also, the exhaust nozzles are molded in two pieces, but not in a way to create a seam as in other Harrier models. Instead the nozzles are molded top half to bottom half.

Aden gun pods are nicely detailed, and if you do not wish to use the gun pods, strakes are provided. Other weapons include two Sidewinder missiles and two Mk-82 500-pound bombs. Surprisingly absent are the drop

The Monogram AV-8A in 1/48th scale is a nice kit.

tanks.

Decals for one RAF GR Mk.1 from No. 1 Squadron and an AV-8A from VMAT-203 are included. In all, this is a very nice kit.

Monogram AV-8B Harrier II, Kit Number 5448
Review and model by Ed Miranda

This is a neatly molded kit of the AV-8B with approximately ninety pieces, including a two-piece canopy. The panel lines are raised, and the canopy glass is clear with no distortions. The cockpit is well done with the side consoles, floor, and rear bulkhead molded in one piece. The instrument panel, stick, and pilot figure are separate pieces.

There is a problem in getting the outriggers to have the proper stance if part number 20, the main gear strut, is incorrectly placed. Make sure it is placed as low as possible into the mating tabs. If not, the main gear will be too long and the outriggers will not sit correctly. Also, wheel well part numbers 25 and 26 need some sheet plastic added to hide gaps when assembled. Care must also be taken in getting the proper alignment of the intakes to the fuselage. There is a potential for mismatching mating parts.

The 1/48th scale Monogram AV-8B builds up into an accurate replica of the real thing.

The exhaust nozzles fit nicely, but need filling of the joint and careful sanding due to external rib detail. The wing halves fit together with a slight mismatch, but fit nicely to the fuselage. However, some filling will be needed on the top rear seam. There is a visible gap on the top wing surface where the wing and outrigger housing meet.

The canopy assembly caused a problem because the canopy is slightly oversized for the mating canopy frame. The windscreen is a good fit to the fuselage.

Weapons and external stores include two drop tanks, two Sidewinder missiles, and two Mk-82 500-pound bombs. Decals for two different AV-8Bs from VMA-331 look good and adhere to the finished model cleanly. The completed model looks good and is an accurate replica of the real AV-8B.

1/32nd SCALE KIT

Revell AV-8A/GR Mk.1, Kit Numbers H-248 and 4718
Comments by Jim Galloway and Bert Kinzey

This is the only model of the Harrier in 1/32nd scale. It has been released two times to date, and only the second issue, kit number 4718 is presently generally available. As originally released (kit H-248), it was molded in light gray plastic, and kit 4718 was molded in olive green plastic. The cockpit consoles have details molded into them, but the instrument panel is represented by a decal. This is unacceptable in this large scale. A control column and a piece with both rudder pedals are also provided for the cockpit. A complete engine is included that can be viewed through the removable access door on top of the fuselage. A linkage allows all four exhausts to move together. Ordnance is very limited with only two gun pods, two rocket pods, and two fuel tanks provided. Strakes may be substituted for the rocket pods.

Surface detailing is represented by raised panel lines. Fit is not as good as it might be, and a good bit of filling and sanding will be required. This is particularly true where the wing meets the fuselage as it seems to be on all Harrier kits. The seams on the exhaust nozzles are very hard to hide. Decals in kit H-248 include markings for AV-8A, 158324, from VMA-513, with a tail code of **WF**. In kit 4718, markings are provided for AV-8A, 159253, from VMA-231. It has a tail code of **CG**.

All-in-all this is not a bad kit considering it was originally tooled ten years ago. If you take the time and make the effort to do it right, this kit can be built into a nice model of the AV-8A Harrier.

1/24th SCALE KIT

Airfix/MPC Harrier, Kit Number
Review and model by Len Salatti

This is the largest of the Harrier kits, both in size and

the number of parts. The total number of parts is an amazing 286, but for its age, as this is a rather old model, there is little flash. The canopy is crisply molded in two pieces, with no mold marks or distortions; however, the canopy is slightly warped and does not fit to the fuselage very well.

The wing tips need a lot of putty to fill in the gaps, and this is the main problem area. Another area of concern is the engine access door, or cover. If building the Harrier with the engine access cover closed, there are gaps along the edges that require filling.

This kit contains a fully detailed Pegasus engine with removable panels, extended ferry wing tips, refueling probe, and complete weapons and stores selection of long range drop tanks, Matra rocket pods, Sidewinder missiles, and 500-pound bombs. Decals are provided for a GR Mk.1 of No. 1 Squadron, and an AV-8A of VMA-513.

The finished kit is impressive due to its size, and takes up a lot of room. It does capture the look of the real

Harrier in profile and sits correctly on its outriggers and main landing gear. This is the only kit of the Harrier in this scale.

The 1/24th scale Airfix AV-8A is the largest model available of the Harrier.

DECAL LISTING

KIT DECALS

Kit	Scale	Type	Number	Unit	Tail Code	Scheme	Comments
Crown No. P831	1/144	AV-8A	158387	VMA-513	WF	Camouflaged	
Takara No. 441005	1/100	AV-8A	159242	VMA-231	NM	Camouflaged	
Hasegawa No. 028	1/72	AV-8A	158389	VMA-513	WF	Camouflaged	
Matchbox PK-16	1/72	AV-8A	159389	VMA-513	WF	Camouflaged	
Fujimi No. 7A-B3	1/72	AV-8A	158950	VMA-542	WH	Camouflaged	Subdued markings
ESCI No. 9051	1/72	AV-8A	156950	VMA-542	WH	Camouflaged	
Italeri/Testors No. 688	1/72	AV-8B	161396	—	—	Camouflaged	FSD #1
	1/72	AV-8B	161398	—	—	Camouflaged	FSD #3
Tamiya No. MA112	1/48	AV-8A	159249	VMA-513	WF	Camouflaged	Blue rudder with white stars
Monogram No. 5420	1/48	AV-8A	159375	VMAT-203	KD	Camouflaged	Red-white-blue rudder
Monogram No. 5448	1/48	AV-8B	162072	VMA-331	VL	Camouflaged	Subdued markings
Revell H-248	1/32	AV-8A	158384	VMA-513	WF	Camouflaged	
Revell No. 4718	1/32	AV-8A	159253	VMA-231	CG	Camouflaged	Subdued markings
Airfix	1/24	AV-8A	158391	VMA-513	WF	Camouflaged	

DECAL SHEETS

Manufacturer and Sheet Number	Scale	Type	Number	Unit	Tail Code	Scheme	Comments
Microscale 72-355	1/72	AV-8A	158949	VMA-542	WH	Camouflaged	Tiger stripe rudder
	1/72	AV-8A	158962	VMA-231	CG	Camouflaged	Blue rudder with white spades
	1/72	AV-8A	158974	VMA-513	WF	Camouflaged	Lt. blue & dark blue rudder
	1/72	AV-8A	158249	VMA-513 Det. A	WF	Camouflaged	Blue rudder with white stars
Model-Decal #15	1/72	AV-8A	158387	VMA-513	WF	Camouflaged	Squad. badge on tail
	1/72	AV-8A	158388	VMA-513	WF	Camouflaged	Alternate scheme
Microscale No. 48-247	1/48	AV-8A	159233	VMA-513	WF	Camouflaged	Lt. blue & dark blue rudder
	1/48	AV-8A	158962	VMA-231	CG	Camouflaged	Blue rudder with white spades
	1/48	AV-8A	158967	VMA-542	WH	Camouflaged	Tiger stripe rudder

Note: Only markings for USMC Harriers are listed.